Rodney's Wife

Rodney's Wife

RICHARD NELSON

THEATRE COMMUNICATIONS GROUP
NEW YORK
2006

Rodney's Wife is published by Theatre Communications Group, Inc., 520 8th Avenue, 24th Floor, New York, NY 10018–4156

This publication is made possible in part with public funds from the New York State Council on the Arts, a State Agency.

TCG books are exclusively distributed to the book trade by Consortium Book Sales and Distribution, 1045 Westgate Dr., St. Paul, MN 55114.

LIBRARY OF CONGRESS CATALOGING-IN-PUBLICATION DATA
Nelson, Richard, 1950-
Rodney's wife / Richard Nelson. — 1st ed.
p. cm.
ISBN-13: 978-1-55936-278-8
ISBN-10: 1-55936-278-2
1. Americans—Italy—Rome –Drama. 2. Motion picture locations—Drama.
3. Jealousy—Drama. I. Title.
PS3564.E4747R63 2006
812'.54—dc22
2006023153

Cover photograph by Cig Harvey
Cover design by Carol Devine Carson
Text design and composition by Lisa Govan

First Edition, October 2006

For Zoe

Rodney's Wife

Production History

The world premiere of *Rodney's Wife* was produced by the Williamstown Theatre Festival (Michael Ritchie, Producer). It was first performed at Nikos Stage on July 7, 2004. It was directed by the author; the set and costume design were by Susan Hilferty, the lighting design was by David Weiner, the sound design was by Scott Lehrer; the stage manager was Leslie Lyter. The cast was as follows:

FAY	Haviland Morris
RODNEY	David Strathairn
EVA	Maryann Plunkett
LEE	Susan May Pratt
HENRY	John Rothman
TED	Tom Sadoski

Rodney's Wife was subsequently produced by Playwrights Horizons (Tim Sanford, Artistic Director; Leslie Marcus, Managing Director; William Russo, General Manager) on December 1, 2004. It was directed by the author; the set and costume design were by Susan Hilferty, the lighting design was by David Weiner, the sound design was by Scott Lehrer; the production manager was Christopher Boll, and the production stage manager was Matthew Silver. The cast was as follows:

FAY	Haviland Morris
RODNEY	David Strathairn
EVA	Maryann Plunkett
LEE	Jessica Chastain
HENRY	John Rothman
TED	Jesse Pennington

Characters

FAY, forty
RODNEY, Fay's husband, late forties
EVA, Rodney's sister, forty-four
LEE, Rodney's daughter, twenty-five
HENRY, Rodney's manager, late forties
TED, Lee's friend, twenty-six

Note: The actress playing Fay also plays
the Woman in the Prologue and at the end.

Setting

1962. A small villa on the edge of Rome.
The kitchen and the living room.

Note: There should be no intermission.

PHAEDRA: What do people mean
when they speak of love?

—EURIPIDES
HIPPOLYTUS

Prologue

WOMAN *(To the audience)*: My mom's name was Fay. She died when I was eighteen. I keep a photo of her on my dresser. She stands in front of a nondescript brick building, wearing a fur coat, looking away.

Recently, my dad passed away, and while cleaning up, I discovered buried in a box of innocuous books—my mom's diary.

Our story is taken from one very long entry.

As I said, her name was Fay, and tonight I'll be her. We're in 1962, in Rome, where she and Dad are spending some of that year. She has just turned forty. And I haven't been born yet . . .

Scene 1

1962. Spring. Early evening. A small villa on the edge of Rome.
The kitchen. Large wooden table, chairs, lamps, etc.
   Distant church bells.
   Fay, forty, attractive, prepares a buffet meal. She is lost in
thought. Sudden laughter from the unseen patio, off. This gets her
attention; she listens, then goes back to work.
   Eva, forty-four, Fay's sister-in-law, comes in, carrying a tray
of half finished drinks from outside, startling Fay when she speaks:

EVA: It's started raining.
FAY: You startled me. What?
EVA: They're coming in. Because it's raining. We'll sit in here?
FAY: But—?
EVA: It's nice in here. I love it. The Italians know how to make a
   kitchen, if nothing else.
FAY: Should I set out—?
EVA: We were going to do buffet. We'll do buffet in here. Let
   everyone serve themselves. Everything looks—lovely.
FAY: Thank you.

EVA: I wish I could cook like—

FAY: I love your cooking, Eva. Tonight I just wanted to do it myself. I'm sorry if I pushed you out.

EVA: No. No. I didn't—and I'm here anyway. You can't get rid of me. *(Laughs at her joke)*

FAY: Why would I want to get rid of—?

EVA: Here they come.

(Sounds of a sudden downpour outside as Rodney, late forties, Fay's husband; Lee, twenty-five, Rodney's daughter; and Ted, twenty-six, Lee's friend, all hurry in out of the rain.)

RODNEY: We just made it! Listen to that.

EVA: It's pouring out there. So we'll eat in—

FAY: Eat in here.

EVA: I love it in here. Romans and their kitchens! You don't see kitchens like this in Tarrytown. Everyone, just grab a— *("plate")*

RODNEY *(Hand on Ted's shoulder)*: You didn't finish—about the—

TED *(Realizing)*: The accident.

LEE: Maybe Ted doesn't want to talk about—

FAY: What accident?

RODNEY: On Ted's way over here, he passed an accident.

EVA *(Handing out glasses from the tray)*: Here are the drinks. The one on the right's— Take that one—

TED: It'd just happened. Obviously. The ambulance wasn't even there yet.

RODNEY: In this country?—

EVA: Rodney. We're guests. *(Smiles, teasing him)*

(Lee stands by Fay. She suddenly fixes Fay's hair, pulling back a few loose hairs.)

LEE: You're sweating.

FAY *(Explaining to the others)*: It's the cooking.

TED: I stopped, but . . . the cars were mangled together. Someone had—he was across the road in a field. Must have gone clear through the windshield. People were—

EVA: So someone was there.

TED: Yes. Shouting: "Over here! There's someone over here!" *(Then explaining)* In Italian.

LEE: Ted knows Italian. *(Lee takes Ted's hand; Fay watches this)* Maybe you don't want to talk about it.

TED *(Not getting the hint)*: I don't mind. When something like that . . . I'm still a bit shaken up.

FAY: Who wouldn't be?

(Short pause.)

LEE *(To Ted)*: Take a plate.

(Plates are passed around, they start to dig into the buffet as:)

EVA: My husband once saw a road accident where someone's head was . . .

LEE: Eva!

RODNEY *(Putting food on his plate)*: The worst accident I ever saw, it was north of San Francisco. I was shooting a movie. Someone—some boy—was driving me to the location. We were on a little hilly road, when the car in front of us— *(Reaches over and puts more food on his plate)*

EVA *(To Ted, "the guest")*: What can I hand you?

TED: I'm fine.

RODNEY *(Continuing)*: —I think to avoid some animal that just ran off the road, swerved; we nearly hit them, but they skidded into the side of the hill, full speed. We were stopped right next to them. *(Stops serving himself)* There was blood all over the inside of their side window. Then before we could get out and help, this car starts to slide back, head down the cliff. It was a straight drop down. No guard rail, nothing. And right in front of me, smearing the blood from

the inside—fingertips struggling to get out, to get the window
or the door or whatever opened. It all happened in seconds.

(Everyone has stopped serving themselves. They are listening.)

And then their car just backs over the side of the cliff and
falls. And . . .

FAY: You saw this?

RODNEY *(To Ted)*: Some things you don't forget. Like that—
(Gestures: fingertips on the window) This may seem funny,
but whenever something goes wrong on a set—

FAY: Which is about every other minute, right? *(Laughs; Rodney
ignores her)*

RODNEY *(To Ted)*: The director may be—whatever. You know
how directors can be. I think—well, I'm not in that car, trying to get out. So how bad could it be.

(Rodney laughs, and the others follow.)

What were we talking about?—

EVA: The accident Ted saw on his way—

LEE: Maybe if we're going to eat we should find a new subject.

TED: I'm sorry, I—

RODNEY: We asked. It's not your fault.

TED: Everything looks so delicious.

LEE: Fay's a real cook.

FAY: I bought three-quarters of it already made, don't listen to her.

TED: If you want, I can show you a few markets that maybe you
haven't—

FAY: I think I'm doing fine. Aren't I?

TED: I'm sorry, I didn't mean—

LEE: Ted's lived here for years, Fay. He knows— *(To Ted)* Don't
mind my stepmother, she likes to discover things for herself.

FAY: What does that mean? I don't. I don't, Ted. If you want to
show me— It was "Ted" wasn't it?

LEE: You know that.

TED: It was. It is.

FAY: It's just that—Ted—we just met. I don't know anything about— *(The others are looking at her)* So—you've lived in Rome for years. *(Takes out a cigarette, then to change the subject, she turns to her husband)* How was today on the set? Everyone—eat. You too—"Ted"? I can remember that.

TED *(To Lee)*: It doesn't matter.

FAY: Assuming you find anything you like.

TED: Everything looks great.

LEE *(To her father)*: Speaking of the set, Dad. *(She puts her arm in Ted's)* Teddy would—

FAY *(Lighting her cigarette)*: "Teddy"??

LEE *(Continuing)*: Teddy would like to visit, if that's possible.

TED: If it's a problem—

RODNEY: You haven't been to Cinecittà Studios! It's like walking—

(Eva finishes:)

EVA: Onto the moon!

TED: I've been, but I thought—

RODNEY *(Not listening)*: Today, Franco—

LEE *(To Ted)*: The director.

RODNEY: I'm keeping a list of the things he says. No one is going to believe me back home.

EVA: Eat. Eat.

(All sit or stand around, plates held or on their laps. And as they eat:)

RODNEY: "Rod, I remain convinced that by far the greatest writer of Westerns—was Homer!" *(Laughs)*

LEE *(To Ted)*: Dad's making a Western. They're making Westerns here now, too.

EVA: Or trying to.

RODNEY: I say: "But Franco would Homer know sagebrush if it bit him on the butt?" Then his mind sort of drifts and he says as he's looking off at this really really fake Western town? Western what? I wonder. More like western Sicily.

I what? I wonder. More like western Sicily I think and he says— I wrote this down: *(Takes out a scrap of paper and reads)* "Shakespeare could have written some real great Westerns just as he wrote some great Italian plays—without ever having been to Italy." What does that mean? *(Laughs and shakes his head)*

TED: I think the point he was making—

RODNEY: I know the fucking point he was making, son! *(Forced laughter)*

EVA: Who's sitting? Who wants to sit?

RODNEY: I'm standing.

EVA: Ted?

RODNEY *(Continuing)*: You've never been to Cinecittà. Incredible.

TED: Actually, I have. I'd just love to see you—

LEE: Teddy was an extra in *Cleopatra*, Dad.

RODNEY: Oh my God!

TED: Anyone could be an extra in *Cleopatra*. They were taking people off the street.

RODNEY: What a mess that was. You know we're still suffering for that. People hear an American accent—

TED: Or a Welsh one.

RODNEY: Right. *(Laughs)* Right. Those fucking bastards. And I mean that literally.

(Laughter.)

(Laughing, shaking his head) People are still owed money.

TED: I was a slave. I forgot to take off my watch.

FAY: What?

TED: If you see the movie—

RODNEY: I won't see it.

LEE: I liked it.

TED: I'm in a crowd of other slaves, and I have my watch on. The man whose job it was to make sure we took off— He missed me.

RODNEY: He was probably drunk. Or feeding his fat face. They don't know what the hell they're doing here. Franco walks around in cowboy boots? Cowboy hat? And glasses. He looks like Yosemite Sam.

TED: Who's—?

LEE: A cartoon character—

RODNEY: These wops don't know for shit. I had to tell them today—

LEE *(Trying to get him to stop)*: Dad.

RODNEY: I can't say "wop"?

LEE: We're in Italy.

RODNEY *(Continuing)*: I had to tell them today—they tried to put these Davy Crockett hats on us—the picture's set on the Mexican border for Christ sake! At lunch, I sat next to some old guy—I don't know what he does there, I don't know if he knows, but he's doing it—forever? He starts talking about the old days. *Quo Vadis*, remember that?

TED: Sure.

RODNEY: How do you remember that? You were a baby.

TED: I saw it somewhere—

RODNEY: He says that during the filming, an extra, a real person, a human being— *(Turns to Lee)* albeit an Italian—was actually eaten by a lion.

EVA: No.

TED: How could—?

RODNEY: I suppose—like your guy who was supposed to be checking the wristwatches on *Cleopatra*—this guy who's supposed to keep the lions here and the extras there, was—? Whatever. I don't know. You don't know what it's like. You should come and watch. You all should come, it's like . . . *(Shrugs)* Who wants a refill? *(As he refills his glass)* This guy, this punk kid from the Morris office here—

EVA: By the way that's where Henry's now. He had to go. I was supposed to tell you.

RODNEY: I know, he called.

EVA: He didn't think I'd remember?

LEE: But you didn't remember, Aunt Eva.

TED: Who's—?

LEE: Henry. Father's new manager.

RODNEY: He'll be back soon. His wife only allows him one drink. She's got him by the balls.

EVA: Rodney! What's this boy going to think he's marrying into?

FAY *(Stunned)*: What??!!

RODNEY *(Continuing)*: And she's not even here. She's three thousand miles away. *(Joking, to Ted)* She's got one hell of a long arm.

EVA: What did this young man from the Morris office—

FAY *(Still stunned)*: What??

EVA: Sh-sh.

RODNEY: He's there to drop off a script. I look at it and nearly strangle him. I say: this is it, son. This is my line in the sand. I shall go no lower in my career than playing a goddamn cowboy in this outpost, but it's a toga picture he wants me to do now. That's the script. I tell him—with these legs?

(Laughter. The punch line.)

We need another bottle.

TED *(Offering)*: Where—?

RODNEY: I'll get it. They paid me in advance. I'm the only one they did pay in advance, in fact, I'm wondering if I'm the only guy on this fucking picture who's been paid. That—would explain a lot.

EVA: I can hear Gerald laughing now.

RODNEY: I can too, Eva. I can, too.

(He goes off to get another bottle. Short pause.)

TED: Gerald??

LEE: Gerald *was* my dad's manager. He was married to Aunt Eva. He recently passed away.

TED *(To Eva)*: I'm sorry.

FAY *(To Lee, still stunned, confused)*: Lee??

LEE *(Ignoring her; to Ted)*: Wow. I'm sorry about that. My father sort of— Sometimes it's hard to even breathe around him. He just sucks up the—

EVA: Don't apologize for your father, Lee. He's a wonderful and generous man. With a lot of character. *(Pause)* He is.

TED: When did your husband pass away?

EVA: Three months ago. My brother—and Fay—were kind enough to invite me . . . He had a wonderful laugh, my husband. That's what Rod was—

FAY *(To Ted)*: How long have you lived in Rome?

LEE: His father's been here for years? Teddy comes and goes.

EVA: It's a beautiful city. My husband would have loved it. He loved to travel. I didn't. I regret that now. That I didn't go with him more. I love the sound of the bells.

(Rodney returns with a couple of bottles.)

RODNEY: I had to wrestle a spider for this. He was this big. *(Shows Eva, who pushes his hand away)*

EVA: Rodney!

RODNEY: Where were we?— Of course, come and visit the set, Ted. I'll show you around myself. I've nothing better to do. *(Laughs and pours)*

EVA: You should feel honored. He hardly ever invites anyone to his set.

RODNEY: I think this is special.

(Fay looks around confused.)

It's stopping out there. We could wipe off the chairs.

EVA: After dessert.

TED: I'm almost there.

EVA: Fay, you haven't eaten anything.

RODNEY: Is anything wrong, Fay? You've hardly said anything.

FAY *(To Ted)*: I'm not a talker. They know that. That's why I get along so well with my husband. *(Smiles; the others laugh)* Why—is everyone so happy? And why is this special? You said— I don't understand.

(The others look at each other, an awkward moment, then:)

LEE: I was going to tell you later. Father knows. We had lunch together today and we told him.

FAY: Told him what?

RODNEY: Lee and Ted are engaged, Fay. It happened last night. Ted proposed.

EVA: On bended knee, I hope.

(Laughter.)

LEE: Not quite.

FAY *(Trying to smile and look pleased)*: Where was this? You said you were going to the movies last night.

LEE: I did.

FAY: With friends.

LEE: Teddy's a friend.

FAY: I was going to go with you. You said I should go. But I didn't want to be around a lot of your young friends. I felt I'd be in the—

LEE: I didn't plan it, Fay. I didn't know what Teddy was planning.

FAY: Have you two thought about this? *(Then)* I didn't mean it that way.

LEE: Fay.

RODNEY: They have. I asked her the same question this afternoon.

FAY: When???

RODNEY: Lee just told you, we had lunch together this afternoon.

LEE *(To Ted)*: At Café Doney. Moravia was two tables away.

TED: I told you he went there.

FAY: Who's Mora—?

RODNEY: You don't care. Trust me.

LEE *(To Fay)*: He writes books.

FAY: So you talked about this at lunch? You've known since—? *(She looks at her watch)* When was someone going to tell me?

RODNEY: We just did. What is the matter with you?

EVA *(To Lee)*: So how did he do it?

FAY *(Suddenly turns to Eva)*: Did you know?

(Short pause.)

LEE *(To Eva, answering her question)*: We were watching—? *(Turns to Ted)* Some movie. I don't remember.

EVA: You should remember. I remember everything about when my husband proposed to me.

RODNEY *(Teasing Eva)*: Was that right after he escaped from the insane asylum?

(Eva pushes him away.)

TED: I hadn't meant to— I was going to wait for some fancy dinner or . . . Then the roof opens up. You hear this grinding of gears—in the middle of the picture. And there's the sky. And stars. And this sort of smack on the face from the fresh air. All the cigarette smoke swirls up. It's like a dream. And so I . . . *(Takes Lee's hand)*

RODNEY *(To Fay)*: Are you sure you're all right?

FAY: Why wouldn't I be? I'm happy like you. *(Turns to Ted)* But I don't know anything about you.

TED: We'll have to fix that.

RODNEY: She's in love with him, Fay. Look at her. She told me all about it at lunch.

FAY: She's told me nothing. Have you?

(Short pause.)

LEE: I should have asked you to come to lunch.

RODNEY: I remember proposing to Fay.

EVA *(To Fay)*: I'm sure you remember that.

FAY: No.

(Rodney laughs.)

RODNEY: I was in Westport doing a show. Something, I don't remember.

EVA *(To Fay)*: Do you remember?

(Fay ignores her.)

19

RODNEY: Fay comes up from the city. She's acting in a show, too, down there.

TED *(To Lee)*: You didn't tell me Fay is also a—

FAY: Was—

RODNEY: I check her into some boardinghouse by the water. Borrow a car, and we go find a beach.

FAY: No one's interested in this, Rodney.

RODNEY: We take a walk. The sun's setting. Like the sky at the pictures I suppose for you. And I say—Lee's what? Now eleven or twelve?

LEE: I was fifteen.

RODNEY: And—this is how romantic I was. *(Smiles)* "Lee needs a mom. She's gone without a mom for long enough." So—Mr. Romantic. *(Laughs)*

FAY: And that's exactly why I'm here—for Lee. *(Reaches out to Lee)*

LEE: I was in boarding school. I hardly ever came home. So don't blame me.

FAY: So I'm something to be blamed for??

LEE: That's not what I meant. You know that. I didn't need a mom. Dad's just saying that.

RODNEY: I thought you—

LEE *(To Ted)*: I was away at schools for—

FAY: For years and years. We know. Don't listen to your father. I don't. *(Laughs)* He's just teasing you. The truth is, Ted, that Lee and I have only really gotten to know each other this year. Isn't that true?

LEE: Yeah.

RODNEY: My daughter, Ted, has finally decided that she likes her family.

LEE: That's not fair.

RODNEY *(To Ted)*: I used to have to bribe her to get her to come home for Christmas.

LEE: That was once. I was seventeen—

RODNEY *("Teasing")*: Now—we can't get rid of her.

FAY: Is that what you'd like, to get rid of—?

EVA: He's teasing, Fay.

LEE: I don't even listen to him.

(This makes Rodney laugh.)

TED *(To Fay)*: So you were an actress?
RODNEY *(To Fay)*: Ted writes.
TED: A wannabee.
RODNEY: He's writing a novel.
TED: Historical fiction? Something about Pompeii.
RODNEY: You've got how many degrees from schools?
TED: I never wanted to leave school. That's what my father always
    accused me of—
LEE: Three or four?
TED: Two.
EVA: We better watch how we speak around him.
TED: No, you don't have to—
EVA: I wasn't being serious. My husband wanted to be a writer.
    He always admired writers more than actors. Except he
    said—as people. He used to say as soon as he made enough
    he was going to become one. He wanted to write detective
    books.
RODNEY: There's money in that.
EVA: Get a couple of drinks in him and he'd start telling you plots
    for his detectives to solve.
RODNEY: And getting a couple of drinks in Gerald was not a dif-
    ficult task.

(Eva laughs.)

EVA: He loved his cocktails. They just didn't love him.
TED *(Changing the subject; to Fay)*: You don't act at all anymore

(Rodney laughs at this.)

FAY: Actually, more than ever. But in private.
RODNEY: Fay was a delicious actress. You should have
FAY: Here I am. My husband doesn't approve of my a

RODNEY: That's not—

FAY: He'd rather I were at his side. But I think he's just scared I'd get a better role than him. Keep competition out of the marriage. There's my advice for the night.

TED: Thank you.

EVA: My husband proposed to me during the war.

RODNEY *(To Ted)*: The Civil War.

LEE: Dad.

RODNEY: She likes it when I tease her.

(Eva doesn't and continues:)

EVA: My husband was passing through Chicago and he's in his handsome uniform. This is before he goes overseas. He went to the Pacific. A lot of islands. He's got only one night. So I lie to my parents and say he can't find a place, he has to sleep on our couch—for the war effort, I tell them. They believed anything. Parents. We wait until they're asleep, and first we start smooching—

RODNEY: How much are you going to tell us? Maybe we don't want to know—

EVA: Young people think we did nothing. Let me tell you, if that couch could talk—it could teach you kids a trick or two. *(Laughs to herself)* I said to him, that night—I want to have your child. So, sure, I'll marry you.

TED: Lee said the same thing to me.

LEE: Teddy!

FAY: Did you? *(To Ted)* How old are you?

LEE: Fay!

FAY: What is wrong with that question?

LEE: He's twenty-six.

TED: And we want to start having children just as soon as . . . *(Turns to Eva)* How many children did you and your husband—?

None.

(Short pause.)

TED *(Quietly to Lee)*: I didn't mean . . .

EVA: My husband couldn't. Not when he came back. *(Suddenly smiling)* Neither does Fay, for that matter. But I think that's been her choice, hasn't it? And that's what makes us such good wives and sisters—because: *(Puts her arm around her brother)* this is my baby here. *(Kisses Rodney on the top of the head)*

FAY *(Putting her arm around Lee)*: And this—is *my* baby—my little stepdaughter. *(Hugs her)*

EVA: You're marrying at the right time, early enough. Like me and Gerald. You marry early and you get to grow up together. So you're not just husbands and wives, just lovers, but—brother and sister. And—at times I was a mother to him, and at times he was a father to me.

(Church bells off.)

I love those bells. I love this city. What I've seen of it.

LEE *(Still being held by Fay)*. You haven't eaten anything.

FAY: I'm not hungry.

LEE: Fay eats like a bird.

FAY *(Nods to Rodney)*: He wants me thin.

RODNEY: Don't blame me. *(Suddenly grabs Fay away from Lee and hugs her. Others respond: "Ohhh!!!")*

FAY *(At the same time)*: How much have you had to drink?

RODNEY *(Grabbing the bottle)*: Not enough. *(Holds up the bottle to Ted)* Ted? Or do you prefer "Teddy"?

LEE: "Teddy's" my name. It's "Ted" to you.

(Ted grabs Lee and hugs her and kisses her on the cheek. Seeing this, Rodney kisses Fay on the cheek.)

FAY: What's that for?

EVA: Shouldn't we go outside?

LEE: Has it stopped raining?

EVA: I think so. I'll check. *(Moves to the door)*

FAY *(To Rodney)*: Come on.

RODNEY: Why do we have to move?

FAY: It's lovely outside.

EVA *(Coming back)*: I just need a towel to dry off the chairs.

LEE: Here's one.

RODNEY: Why are we going outside?

EVA: Come on, get up.

RODNEY *(To Ted)*: Bring that bottle.

EVA: You've had enough.

RODNEY: Bring the bottle.

(Ted picks up the bottle.)

TED: Can I do anything?

RODNEY *(About the bottle)*: You're doing it, son.

FAY: I have little cakes for dessert, I'll set them out. Lee can help me.

TED: Can I—?

LEE: You're the guest.

EVA: I can help—

FAY: I thought you were doing the chairs. Ted, help Eva with the chairs.

(Rodney, Ted and Eva are heading out.)

RODNEY: In and out, why can't we just stay put for five minutes?

(They are off, leaving Fay and Lee. Short pause.)

LEE: What do you want me to do with the cakes? *(Fay looks at her)* This plate all right?

FAY: He's a nice-looking kid.

LEE: Stop it.

FAY: I said nothing, Lee.

LEE: Eva's coming back.

(Eva returns.)

EVA: Where's the bottle we water down? Is this it?

(She takes a bottle, and smells it.)

FAY: You left him with poor "Teddy."

LEE: Teddy can take care of himself.

FAY: Can he? Oh that's good to know.

EVA: How much has Rodney had to drink? Do we know? Was
anyone watching?

FAY: I thought that was your self-appointed job, Eva. Sorry.

EVA: Don't be a bitch. He's filming in the morning. Is that the
dessert? Let me— *("help")*

FAY: Look at our Lee, Eva—getting married. I'm—speechless.

EVA: I think it's wonderful.

FAY: I knew nothing about it. I didn't see it coming. I admit that.

LEE: Neither of you has congratulated me. *(Looks to Fay, then
turns to Eva)* Aunt Eva.

(Lee holds out her arms and goes to Eva who hugs her.)

EVA *(Hugging her)*: Good luck, dear. In marriage you need luck.
(Letting her go) I certainly had my share.

(Lee looks at Fay and goes and hugs her.)

LEE: Aren't you going to say "congratulations"?

FAY *(Hugging her back)*: Congratulations.

EVA *(Setting out the cakes)*: This has made your father so happy.

LEE *(Letting go of Fay)*: Daddy seems really excited about it.

EVA: We all are. *(Turns to Fay)*

FAY: Yeah. *(To Lee)* Why didn't you tell me? *(No response)* He
seems nice. Ted.

LEE: He is.

(As they all set out the cakes:)

FAY: How long have you known—him? *(No response)* How long?
I think as your stepmother, I have a right to ask that. *(To

Eva) Don't I? Your dad, Eva and I have a responsibility to
look after your well-being. Allow me that, Lee. Why did you
say nothing to *me*? You have lunch with your father. Eva
seems to have known . . .

EVA: Rodney thought something was—

FAY: When were you going to tell me?

LEE: Four months.

FAY: Bullshit.

EVA: Fay!—

FAY: We've only been in Rome for five weeks.

LEE: We met in New York.

FAY: What?

EVA: Didn't you know that?

LEE: He followed me here. He came here to see me. His father lives
in Rome, that's true. He knows Rome. But he's here because
of me, Fay.

FAY: Four—months? And you never once mentioned him?

EVA: She mentioned him to me, Fay. And to Rodney. She didn't
say anything to—? *("you")*

LEE: I didn't know how I felt.

FAY: And now you do? Now you know how you feel?

EVA: She accepted his proposal, Fay.

FAY *(To Lee)*: Good for you. That must be nice, to know how
you—

LEE *(Suddenly wiping her hands on a towel)*: I shouldn't leave Ted
alone with—

FAY: But you can leave—us?!

EVA: She's twenty-five years old, Fay! What are you— *(To Lee
who has started to cry)* Why are you crying?

FAY: It's been an emotional day. Leave us alone for a minute, Eva.

EVA: What's the matter?

FAY: Leave us alone.

(Eva hesitates, then starts to go.)

FAY *(To Lee)*: What are you doing?! What are you doing, Lee?—

LEE: I don't know. I don't know.

EVA *(At the door)*: I cried, too. All day. When I got engaged. You sure I can't— *("help")*
FAY: No. Thank you.

(Fay holds Lee's face as she cries.
Henry, late forties, enters from outside.)

HENRY: Oh, I'm sorry. Excuse me, I didn't mean—
EVA: You're not anything, Henry. She's—fine. *(Awkward moment, then)* How was the cocktail party?

(He shrugs.)

HENRY: I don't like to drink.
EVA *(As she goes)*: What a refreshing thought.

(Fay looks up at Henry.)

HENRY: Who's the—? Out there. The guy.
FAY: Lee's—fiancé.
LEE *(Trying to stop crying)*: Ted.
HENRY: Oh that's right. Of course. Rod told me, Congratulations!
FAY: These—are happy tears. *(To Lee)* Aren't they?

(Lee nods.)

HENRY: He looks like a nice boy. What I saw of him. You women cry when you're happy, and you cry when you're sad. One of life's many mysteries—for men. *(Smiles)* I should go call my wife. I usually do that around now. Pardon me. *(Starts to go, stops, then takes out a script from his pocket)* I brought home a script for Rod. It's not an offer. The picture's already shooting back home. Some big shot's not working out, I think, so . . . But Rod should have a look.

(Fay takes the script from Henry.)

FAY: It's already shooting?

(Henry nods, then picks at the food on the table.)

HENRY: So if it happens, which I doubt, we'd have to pick right up and leave, I guess. I think that would be wrong, of course—to leave the Italians in the lurch like that. But—I'm only his manager. His agents seem to think— Well, let's see what happens. But he should read that tonight. Or someone should. He didn't look like he was in a reading mood when I went by. It's a real script and a good part. I have to call home. I'm a little later than usual. And again, my congratulations—marriage is the greatest thing.

(Henry goes off upstairs. Lee takes Fay's hand. Eva enters startling them.)

EVA: Ted would like coffee. I think maybe he suggested it as a hint for your father, who either didn't pick it up or just ignored it.
FAY: Ignored it.
EVA: That's what I think. *(To Lee)* Better? It's lovely out there now. There's a moon.
FAY *(To Lee)*: How romantic. Let's go see the moon.

(Eva stops Fay.)

EVA: Fay, could you help me with the coffee?
FAY: Can't you—?
EVA: We don't want to smother Lee's boyfriend. And you two spend so much time together—you're going to get people talking. *(Laughs)*
FAY *(To Lee)*: I'll stay and help my sister-in-law.
LEE *(Standing)*: I'll take these *("cakes")* out. Maybe Teddy and I will take a walk. I'll bet he's pretty much had it with Father by now.
EVA: I think that's a wonderful idea.

(After a shared look with Fay, Lee goes with the plate of cakes.)

EVA: You need to let her go, Fay. Please. *(Fay stares at Eva)* That's something every mother needs to learn, isn't it? Not that I would especially know about such things. I only guess. And watch. *(Noticing the script that Fay is fingering)* What's that?

FAY: A possible part for Rodney. Maybe. Henry brought it home from his cocktail party with the agents. One of us should read it tonight. *(Hesitates, then hands it to the eager Eva)*

EVA *(As she starts thumbing through the script)*: You and my brother have been so good to me. And don't think I don't know what you're doing.

FAY *(Lost in thought)*: What?

EVA: There are times here, whole—hours—when I don't think of Gerald at all. That's good, isn't it? That means I'm getting better, doesn't it? So—thank you. *(Looks down at the script)* I'll go read this. *(Goes off)*

(Fay, as at the beginning of the scene, is alone.)

Scene 2

Later that evening. Living room. Large table, chairs, lamps, etc. Rodney sits in a chair, staring off, a glass of whiskey-laced milk in his hand.

Fay enters, having put on a handsome blond wig.

RODNEY: So—now you're a blond.

FAY: I felt like being different. *(New thought)* I put it on for you. I know you like me blond.

RODNEY: I like you any way.

(She stops to fix her stockings. She puts a foot on a chair and pulls up her dress. Rodney watches, then:)

Are you flirting with me?

FAY: I was fixing my stocking. Nothing else. Give me a sip. *(She takes his glass of milk and smells)* Where did this cow come from—Scotland?

RODNEY: It's bourbon. From Kentucky. I finally found a place that sells it. *(Fay is distracted, then to say something)* Of course they gouge you. They see you coming. It's like we walk around with a sign—take advantage of me. Where's my sister?

FAY: Probably hanging upside down somewhere.

RODNEY: Fay.

FAY: Check the attic. Is there an attic? I haven't heard her tiptoe-ing around. Why does she do that? Why does she "pretend" to tiptoe?

RODNEY: She doesn't want to be a bother.

FAY: She's failing.

RODNEY: It means everything to her, Fay. She's getting better. You haven't seen her?

FAY: She's in her room reading your script. When I went by her door she must have thought I was you because she looked up. She said, tell you that it's a very good part.

(Rodney nods.)

RODNEY: I know who they're firing, so I know it's good.

(Short pause.)

FAY: You seem upset over this—Teddy.

RODNEY: I'm not. Not at all. Why would you think that?

FAY: She hardly knows him.

RODNEY: They've been seeing each other for months. Did you know that? *(No response)* He's a smart boy. He cares about her.

FAY: So do we.

RODNEY: What does that mean? *(Short pause)* Lee hasn't had a lot of boyfriends, has she? So when she first mentioned this Ted—

FAY: When exactly was this, by the way?

RODNEY: I don't know, weeks ago.

FAY: Really? Then don't you find it strange that you never met him until—?

RODNEY: I've met him many times, Fay. So has Eva.

FAY: What??

RODNEY: Just in passing. Lee'd borrow the car, pick me up, Ted would be there. We've had coffee once or twice. She seems happy, I think there's no denying that. I haven't seen her so happy in . . . *(Shrugs)* Something's been bothering her, I don't know what it is. Adolescence, I told myself. She'll grow out of it—whatever it is.

FAY: She's twenty-five years old—

RODNEY: You should have heard her at lunch today. I don't know why you weren't invited. I told her you've got to share this with Fay. She would be so pleased for you, I said. At lunch, she and Ted talked about having children—

FAY: I heard.

RODNEY: Her face, Fay . . . Thank you God, I think. She was such an unhappy kid. When her mother died . . . I couldn't help. Today I could see her mother in her. *(Looks at Fay)* I'm sorry. I love you, too. *(Goes to her; she smiles, pats him on the shoulder, then turns away)* They're going to stay here. In Rome.

FAY: What????

RODNEY: Once we leave. I said I'd help out. We should, don't you think?

FAY: Why would she stay here?

RODNEY: They're kids. They can't wait to be on their own. I think they even want to be—I don't know—half way around the world from—us. I know I did from my parents. *(Hears something off)* My daughter's back. Now—we need to leave her alone, Fay.

FAY: What do you mean?

RODNEY: Just that. *(Sips his drink)*

FAY: Why did you say that to me?

(Lee enters; Fay and Rodney look at her.)

LEE *(To say something)*: What's wrong with Henry? He's just sitting in the kitchen. He hardly looked up at me. *(To Fay)* I like you blond.

FAY: I know. *(Then back to the earlier question)* Henry called home. His wife's not there. She's always home. He calls every night.

RODNEY: Ted drove back?

FAY *(Before Lee can answer)*: Where does he live?

LEE: The Aventine.

FAY: Is he rich then?

LEE: He's house-sitting. Just for the week. He's not rich.

FAY: And he knows you're not, right? That we're not?

LEE *(Ignoring the question, turning to her father)*: He's picking up a few things. He'll be back.

FAY: Tonight?

LEE: He's staying here tonight.

(Lee can't look at Fay, who turns to Rodney.)

RODNEY: They're engaged, Fay.

LEE: He's driving back.

RODNEY: And she's a woman, she can do what she wants.

FAY *(Trying to smile)*: Can she?

(Rodney takes Lee's hand and holds it proudly.)

RODNEY: It's been a big day. And you seem positively glowing. *(Lee smiles)* My baby.

(Lee leans over and kisses Rodney on the cheek. Then she takes his "milk.")

LEE: Can I? *(Takes a sip and chokes)* What's—? Never mind.

FAY: And he's stayed other nights? Ted?

RODNEY: Fay—

LEE: No. This will be the first.

FAY: But then you've stayed nights at his—

LEE: No. No, I haven't.

(Rodney looks at her.)

RODNEY: I didn't think anyone your age got engaged anymore without—

LEE: I didn't stay a night. But I dropped by during the day.

RODNEY: Ah.

(Short pause.)

FAY: And what sort of other things do you and Ted do?

RODNEY: Leave the girl alone, she—

FAY: I'm interested. I don't know anything about this boy. This man, Teddy. Ted. I just met him. I just learned that there even was a Teddy whom I didn't know anything about.

LEE: We go places. He's taken me to the Colosseum. The Palatine. The Pantheon.

FAY: We went to those places together, too.

LEE: I know. I remember.

FAY: But I'm sure going with him is a lot more enjoyable than going with me. *(Smiles at Rodney)*

LEE: It isn't, Fay.

FAY: Then what do you like about him?

RODNEY: Fay, what are you doing? Why can't you leave—

FAY: I told you, I want to know about this boy!

RODNEY: All you have to do is look at the boy and see why she likes him! And he's smart! He's a writer.

FAY *(To Lee)*: Has he really written any—?

RODNEY: And he treats her well. That's enough. And that's plenty. I like him. A lot.

LEE: I know you do. I know. *(Kisses Rodney on the forehead, then she starts to light a cigarette)* Where's Aunt Eva?

FAY: Upstairs. Reading. Can I have one?

(Lee gives Fay a cigarette and starts to light it for her. Fay holds Lee's hands as she lights. Rodney sees this.)

RODNEY *(To Lee)*: Do you remember, I think you were about three, coming with your mother to visit me in England?

LEE *(To Fay)*: I don't remember.

RODNEY: I've been thinking about it. Because of Henry, I suppose, that's the connection. You were supposed to land early in the morning. So I took a taxi to the airport. When I got there, it said on the board, next to your flight—please go to the desk for information. I remember reading that five, six times: "Go to the desk for information." It was early in the morning. It didn't compute. And then it did. *(Sips his "milk")* And I just started to sweat. I made my way to the desk, and asked the girl there. Your flight, she said, had made an emergency landing. In Newfoundland. Thank God for Newfoundland. Then I said to myself—where the hell is that? No one knows where you're staying. She tells me a woman has been taken to a hospital. What woman? What's her name? They don't know. Did she have a child with her? They don't know. I figure I'll call every hotel if I have to. I get through to information in Newfoundland and learn that there are only three hotels there. I call the first two and no one there has heard of you. Then I call the third. I remember its name: The Albatross Inn. You can't make this up. The Albatross. So I call—and that's where you are. I had found you. I hadn't lost you. You were safe. *(Sighs)* Why did I—? Henry. I know what he's going through— waiting. I know the feeling—like you can't do anything. Right now he's imagining all sorts of awful things that might have happened to his wife. That's only human.

(The phone in the room suddenly starts to ring loudly, startling everyone. Before Rodney gets up, Henry hurries in from the kitchen and answers it.)

HENRY *(Into the phone)*: Hello? Yes. It's Henry. I see. Fine. I said, I see. What time is it there? *(Looks at Rodney)* He's sleeping. I need at least a few hours. I'll wake him up and call back. Fine. Sure. *(Hangs up)* They fired the actor. The part's yours.

LEE: What part??

FAY *(To Rodney)*: You can't take it.

LEE: What part?

(Eva is standing in the doorway, holding the script; she had heard the phone.)

RODNEY *(Seeing Eva)*: I've been offered the part. How is the script?

LEE *(To Fay)*: I don't understand—

EVA *(To Rodney)*: Great. It's what you should be doing, Rod, not some Western in Italy.

HENRY: They need an answer in—

RODNEY: I heard. That was smart to buy some time.

HENRY: You need to start on Thursday.

RODNEY *(Trying to get up)*: What's today?

HENRY: Monday.

LEE: What are you talking about?

HENRY: I told you about it. A new picture for your father. It's shooting in Los Angeles.

LEE: You're going to Los Angeles? When? Fay?

RODNEY: I don't know— I want to read the— *("script")*

LEE *(Sudden outburst)*: You can't go! I don't want you to go. What about the picture you're making? What's going to happen to—?

RODNEY: Lee, this is business. Why are you so upset?

LEE: It's not right!

RODNEY: It happens, Lee. People skip out. Maybe they'll get lucky and put it back together.

LEE: They're counting on you!

RODNEY *(Yells back)*: They'd dump me in a second if they could get someone better! That's how things work, Lee! I don't want to leave you either.

FAY: Neither do I.

LEE *(To Fay)*: You'd go, too? Fay'd go with you?

RODNEY: Of course she would. Fay goes where I go. What would I do without her?

LEE: But I don't want you to go!

FAY: You've got "Teddy." You're engaged.

RODNEY: I'd think you'd want to be away from us. I did with my
   parents. I should take a bath and sober up. And read this
   thing. *(To Eva)* So it's good? *(Has trouble getting out of his
   chair. Eva helps him)*
        (To Lee) You're acting like a child. *(Lee turns away)*
   We're so proud of you.

(Fay starts to move.)

EVA: I'll run his bath, if you'd like.
RODNEY: Fay usually runs my—
FAY: I don't care. Let her.
EVA: I don't mean to get in the way.
FAY: Run his bath, Eva. Have fun!
EVA: What do you mean? *(To Rodney)* What does she mean?
RODNEY: She doesn't mean half the things she says, Eva. Let's go.
   So you think the part's good? What is it? I hope it's not
   another fucking cowboy.

(Eva and Rodney head upstairs.)

LEE *(To Henry)*: What could you be thinking?! He can't walk out!
   He'll never work in Rome again. Have you thought of that?
   It's your job to think of that, Henry!
HENRY: I don't think he'd care. Excuse me. I left my drink in the
   kitchen. *(Goes off, leaving Lee and Fay alone)*
LEE: I didn't expect this. I hadn't thought about this.
FAY: What have you been thinking about, Lee?
LEE: I don't know. I don't want you to go. *(Looks at Fay)*
FAY: I don't want you to get married.
LEE: You're married.

(Henry wanders back in with his drink, interrupting them.)

I should clean up my room for Teddy.
FAY: And maybe put something special on for him? What does he
   like?

LEE *(Suddenly turns):* I didn't ask him to stay! He almost insisted. He said since we've told our parents!—

FAY: Can't you say no?!!!

(Henry, seeing that he is interrupting, starts to go back. Lee stops him.)

LEE: Stay. I'm going. I'll be back down in a few minutes to wait for Teddy.

HENRY: Ted was just pulling in the driveway.

FAY: That was quick.

(Lee, after a look at Fay, hurries outside to greet Ted. Awkward pause.)

HENRY: Where should I wait? . . . Mind if I . . .

FAY: No, Henry. Lee didn't mean—

HENRY: The phone's . . . *(Gestures to the phone)*

FAY: I know.

HENRY: I'm going to call again in . . . *(Looks at his watch)* Soon. Try again.

FAY: I'm sure everything's fine. Your wife's fine.

HENRY: Thank you. *(Church bells in the distance)* The natives are restless, *(Fay looks at him confused)* The natives are . . . like in the movies? It's like we're on the edge of the world, or the empire? I don't think I like traveling. I don't know how you and Rodney have done it all these years. Moving from place to place to place. Isn't it hard not to have a home?

FAY: I have a home.

HENRY: You and Rodney have a place in western Connecticut that you see maybe four weeks a year. That's what he's told me. *(Short pause)* When Gerald was Rod's manager—did he always travel with you two?

FAY *(Her mind on other things):* Usually. But I think that was mostly to get away from Eva. You're smiling. You understand. Now—you've stopped smiling, afraid to offend. Gerald had a lot of women friends, Henry. He liked women. I say—good for him.

(Lee and Ted enter, he carries a small overnight bag.)

TED: I'm back, I hope—

FAY: Look who the cat dragged in, a mouse to play with. I hear you're staying the night, Ted. Welcome.

(She holds out her hand for him to shake; he hesitates, then shakes it.)

LEE *(At the same time)*: I just told him about—he thinks it's a big mistake for Dad to just leave the picture. It's not right.

TED: It could leave a real bad taste in people's mouths here. About Americans. People will lose their jobs.

FAY *(Turns to Henry)*: Henry, what do these kids expect from me?

LEE: Talk to Dad. He might listen to you. Fay—if for no other reason than I don't want you to go.

(Fay looks at Lee, then:)

FAY: Ted, have a drink. Catch up. Pour yourself what you want, I don't feel like getting up.

HENRY *(Moving to get drinks)*: What would you like?

LEE *(Nearly shouting)*: Did you hear me, Fay?! I don't want you to go.

FAY *(Suddenly erupts at her)*: I don't want you to go either! But what can I do?! When do I ever get what I want?! So you're talking about having children. Your father's so pleased I thought he'd burst a—

TED: I think we'd both like to start a family as soon as—

FAY: Shut up. —I'm sorry. It's just that I wasn't talking to you.

LEE *(To Henry)*: Is there a glass for Teddy?

HENRY: I'll get one from the kitchen.

(Henry goes off toward the kitchen.)

FAY *(To Ted)*: I said: Sorry. So—do you like me as a blond, Ted? You haven't said anything.

TED *(After a look at Lee)*: It's nice. It's good.

FAY: And Lee? You like me as a blond, don't you?

LEE: I told you that. I've already complimented you.

> *(Fay nods. Henry returns with a glass and pours Ted a drink.)*

FAY *(To Ted)*: Henry's waiting for his wife to get home. She's supposed to be home. He's worried.

HENRY: I'll try again in ten minutes. *(Looks at his watch)*

FAY: Give her time. Why don't you sit down. *(Then to Ted, referring to his bag)* Are those your—overnight things? *(Ted nods)* Let me guess. Toothbrush. Underwear. Clean socks. Pajamas.

> *(Awkward pause.)*

My husband takes forever in the bath. He's like the cliché of a woman.

HENRY: He's reading the script.

> *(Short pause.)*

FAY: I wonder if Eva is in there with him. We know she'd like to be.

LEE: Fay.

FAY: I'm sorry. I forgot we have a guest. *(Turns to Ted)* Ted, ever since the unfortunate demise of Gerald—the situation if not the cause of his untimely passing, by the way, required of my husband, Eva's brother, some tact as well as skill in hiding all from Eva, such as getting the underpants back up over the rather stiff corpse, and getting said corpse out of the young woman's boudoir, but that aside, what was I saying?—ever since this, my sister-in-law has, let us say, added her older brother, my husband, to her pantheon of men, there beside the blessed and good Gerald. She looks at him like a hungry puppy to its master. Rodney doesn't object.

Though he does think I'm jealous. But Lee knows better.
Don't you.

LEE: I don't think you're jealous of Eva, no.

(Pause.)

FAY: Should we have some food while we're waiting?
TED: What are we waiting for?
FAY: For Henry to make his call. We can't leave him—
HENRY: You don't have to sit up with me.
FAY: Please. We insist. Don't we. And besides we don't have any-
thing better to do.

(Short pause, then:)

LEE *(To Ted)*: We're waiting to talk to Dad.
FAY *(Out of the blue)*: Henry, do you think I'm still attractive? *(No
one knows what to say)* Don't wait too long.
HENRY: Of course.

(Fay pulls up her skirt a bit.)

FAY: Do I still have nice legs? Teddy?
TED: I said to Lee earlier, how attractive I thought you were.
FAY: And what did Lee say?

(Short pause, then:)

LEE: That I think your legs are beautiful.
TED *(To Lee)*: You didn't say anything about her—
LEE: I must have. I'm sure I did.
FAY: Tell me about yourself, Ted.

(Ted looks to Lee who nods, then:)

TED: I—
FAY: You need her approval?

TED: I don't know what you want to know.

FAY: Your father's a . . . ?

TED: Writer.

FAY: Ah. Your mother?

TED: They're divorced. I rarely see—

FAY: Stepmother? *(To Lee)* They're the worst, aren't they?

TED: No. Not yet.

(He smiles.)

FAY *(Very "polite")*: Why do you smile?

TED: Well, my father's very—he's shy. But there is a woman near where we—

FAY *(Interrupting, turns to Henry)*: Henry, could you get us something to eat from the kitchen? Biscuits. Cheese. Anything. My stomach's beginning to feel a little funny.

LEE: You didn't eat dinner.

FAY: So that's why. *(Turns back to Ted, as Henry goes out)* And is there anything you'd like to know about me? Now that I know about you? Or do you know everything?

LEE: No. He doesn't.

TED: Not that she doesn't talk about you pretty much all the time.

FAY: And what does she say?

(He hesitates then:)

TED: That—and I hope I'm not speaking out of turn—she thinks you have this vast well of talents. And she hopes one day you're going to find—the right thing.

FAY: The right thing? I've tried lots of "right" things.

TED: I know. She—

FAY: I am the Queen of Hobbies, Teddy. And if we go to Los Angeles tomorrow, next month—what does it matter— I will learn to do something. Maybe ride a horse. I hate horses. They scare the hell out of me. But I'll learn to ride a horse in Los Angeles. So that's settled. Just like I learned to paint— somewhere. Where was that? If you can call filling in those numbers painting. But I do. I've learned to knit. And draw. And cook. And bind books from some prop guy on some set somewhere. I wasn't paying attention.

(Henry returns with a plate of biscuits and cheese.)

(To Henry) You've sliced the cheese, dear? You should let us do that. This isn't America. *(Turns back to Ted)* What I think Lee's really worried about—

TED: I didn't say she was worried.

FAY: Is that I'm alone. That I'll be alone. Her father, you see, always says he can't socialize with people from work, it confuses things he says. I understand. So we go to these places, and who do we meet? We're only there for . . . Depends on the size of his role. We meet people in the business. So we don't see anyone. I don't. And now there's Eva too.

TED: She seems nice.

FAY: Does she? Oh. And it all makes for a—what? A very close family, Ted. You should know that before enlisting.

TED: I sense that. And admire it. Even a little jealous.

FAY: Don't be. Trust me.

(She laughs. This makes Lee laugh.)

TED: Why is that . . . ? *("funny")*

FAY: It's private. *(Then changing the subject)* While we're asking each other questions, how are the "intimate" relations between you two?

LEE: Fay.

FAY: I'm sorry I thought we were getting to know each—

(The phone suddenly rings, startling everyone. Henry picks it up.)

HENRY *(Into phone)*: Hello? *(To the others)* It's my wife. *(Into phone)* I've tried to call . . . where have you—? *(Listens)*

EVA *(Hurrying from upstairs)*: Rod loves the script so far! He says he hasn't been offered a part like this in ages—

LEE: No. Fay? *(To Eva)* Is he out of the bath? *(Eva nods. To Ted)* Let's go talk to him. Come on. Come! He can't do this! Dad!?

(She runs up the stairs, Ted follows.)

EVA *(To Henry)*: It's a comedy. He has—

HENRY *(Gesturing to the phone)*: My wife.

EVA *(To Fay)*: He hasn't done a comedy in years. Has he? I always thought he should do more comedies. When he was a boy he could mimic anyone. He'd go through each of our teachers, one by one, first Mr. Sullivan, the math—

FAY: Be quiet! Just stop talking! I just don't want to hear—

EVA: I'll go clean up the kitchen.

FAY: It's cleaned up. Eva! I'm— Sorry.

(She is gone. Henry hangs up the phone and explains to Fay, whose mind is somewhere else.)

HENRY: The car had broken down on the Henry Hudson. She's fine. *(Laughs to himself)*

FAY: What?

HENRY: Nothing. Something between us. *(Lying)* I think it's all a big plot to buy a new car. She wants a station wagon.

FAY: Sure. Women are sneaky like that.

HENRY *(Ignoring her)*: I said, first—it's Westchester, then it's a station wagon. *I* liked West 78th myself. But maybe she's right. *(Suddenly thinking)* How did she get this number? I must have left it. That's right—I gave it to her. I remember.

(Lee wanders in, confused.)

LEE: He loves it. You're leaving tomorrow. He's packing. *(Dazed, she wanders off again)*

HENRY: So much for doing the "right" thing.

FAY: And what is that?

HENRY: I don't know. They're going to go crazy. The Italians. I don't know. I better pack myself. We're going home. My wife will be pleased. I didn't mention . . . I'll surprise her.

FAY: You won't go to California with—?

HENRY: I'll go home first. *(Starts to go. Fay is distracted. He stops; it just comes out)* She's expecting. My wife. No one knows. We promised not to tell— Not yet. She felt the baby kick, that's why I was smiling. You asked why I—? I don't know why I'm telling you. See why I was so worried? *(Big sigh)* What a night. *(Goes. Fay turns back to where Henry left)*

FAY *(Having heard nothing)*: I'm sorry, what?

(Ted enters from upstairs; he goes to pick up his bag, then starts to head to the kitchen and out of the house.)

What are you doing?

TED: She's upset. She wants to be alone tonight. I can understand that. I'd feel the same way. *(Shakes Fay's hand)* Thank you for dinner. I'll be back in the morning and help you get off. Goodnight.

(He goes. Pause. Fay is alone.)

FAY *(To herself)*: Goodnight.

Scene 3

Later that night. It is raining outside. Living room. Eva sits, writing notes to herself. A single lamp is lit. After a moment, Rodney, in his robe, enters behind her with a script. He touches her shoulder, startling her:

EVA: Ahh!

RODNEY: I'm sorry. Where's Fay?

EVA: What are you doing up?

RODNEY: Where's my wife? I came down to find her. I was afraid she'd fallen asleep down here.

EVA: She's not in your room?

(He looks at her: Of course she isn't.)

Maybe she took a walk.

RODNEY: It's raining again.

EVA: You must be exhausted. What time do we have to get up?

(He shrugs. Short pause.)

Have you tried Lee's room?

(Short pause.)

RODNEY *(Without looking at Eva)*: Why would she be in Lee's room? Ted's here with my daughter—
EVA: He didn't stay.
RODNEY: What?
EVA: She asked him not to. Because we're leaving, she said. She . . .
RODNEY: But they just got engaged. What does it matter if we're leaving—
EVA: That's not how fathers are supposed to talk. *(Smiles)*
RODNEY: No. I suppose . . . *(Then)* She could be out for a walk. It's just drizzling. Her last night in Rome.
EVA: It's pouring rain out there, Rod. Go back to bed. *(He doesn't move)* She's probably in Lee's room. *(He doesn't look at her)* She sometimes sleeps in there—on the couch?
RODNEY: On the couch? Does she? I suppose my snoring . . .
EVA: I know when Gerald snored, I used to go downstairs to the rec room and sleep. About two flights away. I could still hear him. *(Smiles. Rodney nods)* So—it's normal.
RODNEY: It is. But I still don't see why Ted couldn't spend the night—
EVA: You could probably go and wake her and—I doubt if they lock the room. Why would they do that? *(She starts to put aside her writing)* I could go if you'd like—
RODNEY: No. Let her—sleep. She hasn't been sleeping. She needs to rest. *(Eva sits back down)*
EVA: I can't sleep either. I've been sitting here making lists. If we're really leaving tomorrow—
RODNEY *(Not listening)*: I'd hardly call that a couch in Lee's bedroom. More like a big chair. How can Fay sleep on that? You've seen her? Sleeping in that chair?
EVA: She told me. One morning I saw her come out—and she told me she'd slept the whole night on Lee's couch.
RODNEY: I feel like a monster making her—I'm the one snoring, I'm the one who— What is wrong with that boy? I would have stayed!

(Short pause.)

EVA: Why don't you go back to bed?

(No response.)

I'll pour you a drink.

(She gets up and goes to the table where the bottle and glasses have been left.)

(Holding up a glass) Is this yours? Lipstick. *(Looks at another glass)* Lipstick. *(Another)* Here's a man's glass. *(As she pours)* Will we be coming back for the wedding? Ted and Lee's wedding?

RODNEY: I'm encouraging them to elope.

(Eva nods and hands him his drink.)

Once they're married we can bring them back to the States and we can have a party or something. But let's get them married. *(Smiles)* They're in love.

EVA *(Sitting back down)*: They are. *(Rodney's mind is somewhere else)* Gerald didn't want a wedding either. I made him. Tricked him into it, remember? And you remember who my matron of honor was? She looked so beautiful—holding little Lee in her arms. God I miss your wife. *(Suddenly)* And I didn't mean that as a criticism of Fay—I just miss her.

(Rodney nods, then:)

RODNEY *(Holding up his glass)*: And I miss your husband.

EVA: You do?

RODNEY: I miss being able to say to him, "Gerald, will you tell my sister to shut up." And he would.

(She reaches over and "hits" him.)

EVA *(Not meaning a word)*: You haven't changed since you were eight. I hated it when you teased me then and I hate it now. You know it's very unattractive.

(He shrugs, then suddenly "messes up" her hair.)

Stop that! Stop it! Grow up!

(She smiles at him; she enjoyed that. He sits down and sips his drink.)

I would have thought Lee'd want a wedding with Fay as *her* matron of honor. They've become so close.

(Rodney doesn't respond.)

Henry's doing a very good job, isn't he?

RODNEY: Yeah.

EVA: I like him so much. Gerald would have approved.

RODNEY: It's nice to hear you say that.

EVA: What a nice man. He was so worried about his wife. He calls her every day? I didn't know men did that. Gerald always talked abut how expensive long distance was.

RODNEY: It is.

EVA: And how—difficult to get through. It didn't seem to be that hard.

RODNEY: Sometimes it can be.

EVA: I can't believe Henry who seems so responsible about everything else could just go to bed like that. There's so much to do if we're leaving tomorrow. I hope he's not thinking that I'll—

RODNEY: Knowing Henry, he's probably upstairs right now making lists.

EVA: He's asleep. His light's out. I noticed when I went to the bathroom. I listened at his door and heard him breathing.

RODNEY: Did you listen at my daughter's door and—?

EVA: I don't think they were asleep. *(Pause)* It was a big day. Huh? Probably hasn't sunk in yet, but give it time—it's not every day that a father sees his only daughter—only child—get engaged. No wonder you can't sleep. And now this movie . . . It'll be hard to leave them, won't it?

(He looks up at her.)

RODNEY: Maybe this isn't the right thing to do.

EVA: What isn't?

RODNEY: Walking out on the people here, out of the picture. *(Fiddles with the script)* I was lying in bed thinking . . .

EVA: You were asleep. I heard you snoring. Which is why your wife had to go and sleep in—

RODNEY: I woke up.

EVA: In your daughter's room. On the couch.

RODNEY: I was reading through this *("script")* again. Maybe I shouldn't have, but I looked at it again. Maybe it's not as good of a part as we thought.

EVA: It's a wonderful part. You'll be—

RODNEY: You can read this in a way and see that my character's not all that central to much of anything. Maybe the actor wasn't fired, maybe he walked, Eva.

EVA: Henry said he was fired.

RODNEY: What does Henry know except what he's told? People lie, Eva. They hide things. How useful is my character? Look at it that way and you see how at the end of things, how much of him could be cut. It's probably being cut now. How many other actors have been offered the part? Actors who aren't in the middle of a fucking cowboy movie in the middle of Italy? Actors not so desperate?

(Short pause.)

EVA: You're going to be wonderful. You are a wonderfully funny actor. You always do this, you know. Gerald used to laugh about it.

RODNEY: Do what?

EVA: "Every time your brother gets offered a job," he'd say this, "he puts himself through hell before he takes it. 'Is it right for me? Can I do it? Is there something better?' 'For Christ sake, Rodney,' I'd tell him—'cash the check.'"

(She laughs, this makes Rodney smile and then onto a new more confident thought:)

RODNEY: Today—the director? He really makes me laugh, Eva. We're supposed to be watching a boat go down a river. He says, look at me, I'm a boat! I'm a boat! And we watch him fall right into the river.

(She laughs a little too hard, trying to be helpful.)

EVA: "I'm a boat!"

RODNEY: It's about up to his chest. He stands: "I'm a boat!" They know how to have a good time. They enjoy making movies. I appreciate that. They may be shit movies, but they have fun. The entire set of this picture, this cowboy—it looks like we're in Sicily! *(Shakes his head and smiles)*

EVA: I'm sure you helped.

RODNEY: I try, Eva. I really do. I try to help. But I can't wait to get home. It's hard to feel real here. Hard to feel you're not alone.

(He hears something.)

EVA: The wind. Or the rain.

RODNEY: I heard a voice.

EVA: The rain.

RODNEY: I like this boy Ted.

EVA: Me, too.

RODNEY: He was telling me about his book he's writing? It's a normal day in the life of this family back in— *(Shrugs)* Way back. And the volcano erupts in Pompeii. He's done a lot of work. He says that even now they're discovering whole rooms—that just sort of stopped. One minute normal and then . . . *(Snaps his fingers)*

EVA: So he has to stay here to work on his book.

RODNEY: He does.

EVA: That'll be good for Lee. For the two of them just to be alone. No—distractions. It isn't until you're alone that you can even feel like—a couple. When Gerald and I were first alone—after getting married—it wasn't until then that we really got to know each other. That's when a marriage starts, a life together. What's Fay going to do in L.A.? Do you know?

(He shrugs, then:)

RODNEY: She's been talking about learning to ride. It's something she hasn't done yet.

EVA: Really?

RODNEY: She's scared of horses and so she thought it would challenge her.

EVA: Good for her.

RODNEY: You're a good rider.

EVA: I am. I can help her.

RODNEY: That's what I was thinking.

EVA: I can keep an eye on her.

RODNEY: That's what I'm thinking.

(He fiddles with the script.)

This so-called Western, no one's ever going to see it.

EVA: I doubt it.

RODNEY: They can just put another guy in my place for the rest of the movie. No one will even notice. They dub everything anyway.

EVA: They'll be okay.

RODNEY: The director told me the other day: He wants to show the real cruelty of the West. What's behind those grinning

white American teeth? Why was he telling me this? I felt
almost like a traitor.

EVA: Now you're going home.

(He nods.)

You're a good person, brother. You are. Maybe too good.

(She goes behind him and hugs him.)

And that is your burden, and sometimes your problem.

RODNEY: What do you mean?

EVA: I remember Mom and Dad always saying—this is when you
had just gone off to college—Rodney is too nice. He wor-
ries about other people too much. He wants to be good.
They thought—I suppose, they were afraid you'd get hurt.
Be taken advantage of. Be used. *(Short pause)* Your wife
shouldn't be sleeping on a little chair. I'm going to tell her
to move. *(Moves away)* That she can go back to her bed
because you've stopped snoring. Or she can come down
here and keep her husband company, because he can't sleep.
(Looks at him) Do you mind if I do that? *(No response)* You
don't? Excuse me.

(She goes. Pause. Rodney sits very still.
Then Eva returns from upstairs.)

RODNEY *(Without looking at her)*: Was she in there? *(Eva nods)*
Was she on the couch?

(No response. She sits. Fay enters, buttoning up the night-
gown she has just thrown on.)

FAY *(Entering)*: What's going on? Rodney, you want to see me?
What time is it?

RODNEY: I'm sorry if I was snoring.

FAY: What??

RODNEY: Wasn't I snoring? *(Looks at her)* I'm asking you: Was I snoring?!!!

FAY: What are you talking about?

(Rodney stands up, glass in hand.)

RODNEY: I need some milk.

EVA: Let me get—

RODNEY: No. *(Finishes his drink)* My stomach feels a little . . . Maybe milk . . .

EVA: I could make you something to eat. It might help. Or Fay could. Fay, make Rodney something to eat!

RODNEY: No. No.

(He goes off to the kitchen.)

FAY: What's happening? What's wrong with my husband? Why can't he sleep? What have you told him, Eva? I don't understand.

EVA: I think you do. Why don't you finish buttoning up, or would you like some help?

(She tries to help, Fay pushes her hands away.)

FAY: You evil nosy little woman. Why didn't you knock?

EVA: So it's my fault?

FAY: You could have knocked.

EVA: Why didn't you lock the door?

FAY: They don't have locks!

EVA: Oh. I didn't realize that. I'm sorry.

FAY: You should have knocked! What did you tell him?!

RODNEY *(Entering with his milk)*: About what? She's told me nothing. Is there something to tell? By the way I thought young Ted was staying the night with Lee.

FAY: I suppose he changed his mind.

(Rodney pours bourbon into his milk as:)

I didn't know anything about that. Ask your daughter.

(He looks at her.)

Go ahead, ask her. I've done nothing, Rodney. What did she say she saw? I sleep sometimes in your daughter's room because—ah! Now I see why you were asking about the snoring. Yes. Yes, you were snoring. *(Tries to smile)* Maybe you should see someone about that. *(Another effort at a smile)* I was cold. I forgot to bring a blanket with me, and I didn't want to go back and risk disturbing you, so . . . Lee only has the one blanket. She was nice enough to share it. What am I being accused of?

(Eva goes to her and again tries to button the buttons Fay has missed.)

EVA: Button up, dear. As you said, it's cold.

(Fay pushes her away again.)

FAY: I can do that.
EVA: Who said you were being accused of anything? Rodney can't sleep. He's your husband. Keep him company. Why is that a big deal?

(Short pause.)

FAY: Oh. I'm sorry. I misunderstood. I thought— Never mind what I thought. *(She goes to Rodney; gently)* Why can't you sleep? You need a pill? I have some upstairs. But how much have you had to drink tonight?
EVA: She *was* on the bed, Rodney, not the couch. And neither had any clothes on.

(Fay stands up, having been blindsided by Eva.)

FAY: Now what do we do?

(The phone suddenly rings. They ignore it; it rings a few times more.)

The phone . . .

(Eva goes to answer it.)

EVA *(Into the phone)*: Hello? This is his sister . . .

(She listens. Henry, putting on his robe, appears in the doorway.)

(To Henry, explaining) Los Angeles. They have flights tomorrow.

(Henry takes the phone and talks, writing down the information. As he does, Lee, half-dressed, appears in the doorway. Eva notices her first, then Fay, then Rodney, who can't look at his daughter.)

FAY *(To Lee, explaining)*: Los Angeles.
HENRY *(As he hangs up)*: They've booked a morning flight. We'll have to be at the airport by—
LEE: What's going on? Fay, what's—?
EVA *(Yells)*: Get out of here, Lee! Go back to bed! Do you hear me?!
LEE *(Fighting back)*: Don't talk to me like that! I'm not a child! Leave me alone! You hear me, leave me alone!!
FAY *(At the same time)*: Lee. Lee. Don't, Lee. Don't.

(Fay grabs Lee, holds her from behind, keeps her from attacking Eva, strokes her arm to calm her down. No one knows what to say, then:)

HENRY: So the plane's at nine. They expect you on the set by eight, Rodney, so I'll call and say what? You're sick? We shouldn't tell them anything until we're out of here?

EVA: That's right, Henry. Good thinking. You sound like Gerald now.

(No one has anything to say.)

HENRY *(Looks at his watch, then)*: My God, we better get some sleep. Look at the time. You all must be exhausted.

(No response.)

Goodnight.

(He goes off to bed.)

FAY *(To Lee)*: You go, too. Go on.

(She strokes Lee's arm, then kisses her on the forehead.)

LEE: I don't want you to go tomorrow, Dad. I'm begging you not to go.
FAY: This isn't the time—
LEE: What happened?
EVA: I'll take her. Come on. Come with me.

(Lee looks at Fay:)

FAY: Go with Eva, Lee. Please.

(Lee starts to go with Eva.)

LEE: I don't want you to—
EVA: That's enough. *(Turns to Rodney)* Rodney—wherever Mom and Dad are—I'm sure they're still worried about you.

(She leaves with Lee. Short pause.)

FAY *(Suddenly remembers, calls)*: Goodnight, Lee!

LEE *(Off)*: Goodnight!

(Fay makes a move to leave.)

RODNEY *(Shouts)*: Stay in here!!!!

(Fay looks at him, then nods.)

FAY *(Calmly)*: I'll be right back. I'm just going to the bathroom.

(She goes. Off, a dog barks. Rodney listens, straightens his robe and pajamas and waits. Fay returns wearing a robe now over her nightgown.)

You want more light on?

(No response. She doesn't turn on another light. She stands looking at him, then:)

I can't imagine what you're thinking. I'm sorry. I ee's your daughter. But it is not what you probably . . . Whatever. I don't dare try and get into your head. I know I wouldn't succeed. I suppose I owe you some sort of explanation. That's not the word. "Reason"? I don't know. *(He stares at her)* I have always gone with men, Rodney. You know that. You've met some of them, my old "boyfriends." You've even made fun of them. We have. *(Smiles)* I think you've even been jealous . . . *(He continues to stare at her)* What do you want to know? Do you want me to stop talking? Do you want me to go away? *(He shakes his head)* Good. *(Thinks, then)* This did not— I'd never been with a woman—before. Though now I see I've had crushes. I suppose I didn't even know that was a choice for me. *(He looks at her)* "Choice" isn't the right word either. When I think back on it, some of these crushes were pretty serious. And I seriously—fought them? Repressed them? Lied to myself about them? Backstage stuff. Dressing room stuff. If you don't want to . . .

(He looks at her) Lee—on the other hand, had. With a
woman. With women. She was the experienced one. I'm not
blaming her. *(Smiles)* By no means. And there is nothing to
blame. That's not why— She's been the . . . She's held my
hand. Which, I tell you, Rodney, has certainly needed holding. *(Sighs)* I've dreaded this moment. Be strong, Fay. *(Takes
a deep breath, then)* This boy, Ted, it's all wrong. I can
promise you that. It's not fair to her. It's not fair to him.
RODNEY: She loves him.
FAY: No.

(Short pause.)

No. Now maybe she loves the idea of making you happy.
I think maybe that. That makes sense to me. *(Shrugs)* How
much have you—pushed them together? How much—is
you? That's just dawning on me now.
RODNEY: Do you love her?

(Pause.)

FAY: I didn't expect you to ask me that. But thank you for it.

(Fay starts to cry.)

RODNEY: Did you put that wig on for me or her?
FAY *(Through her tears)*: What?
RODNEY: The blond wig. For me? Or her?

(She just looks at him. No response. He looks away.)

When you flirt with me are you acting?
FAY: When do I flirt with you?
RODNEY: All the time!
FAY: I don't know. Good question.
RODNEY: When we got married Lee was a kid—
FAY: Fifteen.

RODNEY: Fifteen. Did . . . ?

FAY: It didn't happen then. I swear to God. It's recent, Rodney. Months. Until then I was your normal typical uncaring, thoughtless, self-involved stepmother. I promise. *(Smiles, then)* And then. Then. And then—I wasn't. I won't bother you with how that happened. I've already said—Lee guided me. She knew about us—before me. But you can't tell me you didn't guess something was different. *(Smiles again)* I certainly felt I was— That it was obvious just to look at me.

RODNEY: When we got married, you loved me. *(She looks at him)* And now I disgust you.

FAY: You don't—disgust me. If that's what you've been feeling I'm—I didn't mean to hurt you.

RODNEY *(Suddenly shouts)*: You could have fooled me, Fay!!

FAY: I don't want to turn this into a shouting match! If you just want to shout at me, go ahead and shout! *(Short pause. To keep talking)* Eva obviously was guessing something. She's hovered around like a . . .

RODNEY: Hawk?

FAY: I think "vulture" was the bird I was looking for. But, okay, hawk.

RODNEY: She's trying to protect me.

FAY: From what?

RODNEY: She thinks I'm too—good. Tonight I heard you two in bed. I've just been realizing that it was you. I'd thought it was "Teddy." Can't you cheat better?

FAY: It was our last night together. We were thoughtless.

(She shrugs.)

RODNEY *(Interrupting)*: What do you think of Ted? We haven't talked about any of that since the big news. He seems like a nice boy. A little young—emotionally—to get married, I'd have thought. Lee's young that way herself, so as a parent you worry, but I think they'll find a way to make it work. I feel pretty good about that.

FAY: Rodney.

RODNEY: I feel it's the right thing.

FAY: What are you talking about?

RODNEY: They're getting married, Fay. You can't stop that! They're going to elope.

(He smiles and sits back. Short pause.)

FAY: But now *you* mean to hurt *me*.

RODNEY *(Sips his drink)*: She'll get married. Like you are. *(Smiles at her)* She'll have children. She'll grow up. This is over. Do you understand? *(No response)* Now if you plan to leave me . . .

FAY: And go where? I don't know what to do. Something's got to happen. I know that. I just don't know what.

(He takes another sip, then:)

RODNEY: When my mother was dying, Fay—she asked me to promise that her body would be cremated and her ashes thrown into the sea. Some sea. Any sea. She didn't care. I said, have you talked about this with Father? And she had, but he wanted to bury her in the family plot in Ohio. He'll fight for that, she said, so promise me, Rodney, that I'll be cremated. Promise me. And I promised. And she died. And she's buried in my father's family plot in Ohio. He wanted that. And when I argued with him, Fay, he said—he wanted to know he could be beside her forever. He wanted her next to him, and now—since he died, she is. What she wanted— it hurt him, Fay. And all he wanted was to lie for eternity next to the woman he loved. What is wrong with that?

FAY: It was her body.

RODNEY: Not after she was dead.

(Short pause.)

FAY: And what was your sister's part in all this? What side did she take?

RODNEY: Eva didn't care just as long as there was room in the plot for her.

FAY: And you.

RODNEY: And me.

FAY: And what about me? Will I be wedged into that family huddle as well?

(He shrugs, then:)

RODNEY: That has been my hope. With Lee's mother on one side of me, and you on the other.

FAY: A position I think I'll have to fight Eva for.

RODNEY *(Smiles)*: Maybe.

FAY: So—cremate me.

RODNEY: Is that what you'd like?

FAY: Sure.

RODNEY: We'll see.

(Pause.)

FAY: Will I be going to Los Angeles with you tomorrow?

RODNEY: You're my wife.

(Short pause.)

FAY: And will Eva be staying with us there too? *(He nods. She "smiles")* Good. Is it still raining out? *(No response)* Are we going to stay up all night?

RODNEY: You're not the woman Lee's mother was. That was love.

FAY: I'm not sure it was, Rodney. I'm sorry I never got the chance to meet her. Know her. I'm sorry she died. Lee often talks about—

RODNEY *(Yells)*: Shut up about Lee! Everything with you comes back to Lee! I'm talking about my wife! *(Suddenly bangs his chest)* I lost my wife!

(Stares at her) And then I met you. I saw you acting. What an actress you were. Gerald took me to the show. He was seeing some really stupid girl.

FAY: She was really stupid. I had to act with her.

RODNEY: He said he wanted to draw me out of myself. He said I should see this girl—woman. And so—you walked out on stage, and sat in a chair, like no one's ever sat in a chair before, I said to myself. You had the most beautiful legs. Have. Still do.

FAY *(Smiling)*: You always said—my legs were the best part of my acting.

RODNEY: I only ever said that in bed. *(Looks closely at her)* Why did you put that on?

FAY: What?

RODNEY: The robe. You didn't have the robe on before. You go to the bathroom and you come back in a robe.

FAY: It's cold.

RODNEY: You're sweating. Why do you need to cover up?

FAY: You want me to take the robe off, Rodney? *(Laughs)* This is ridiculous—

RODNEY: Yes.

FAY: No.

(Rodney starts to cry.)

RODNEY: Take off the goddamn robe.

(She hesitates, then stands and takes off the robe, she fiddles with her nightgown, and sits back down.)

FAY: There. Happy? How drunk are you?

(He stares at her, then:)

RODNEY: Why haven't *we* had a baby, Fay?

FAY *(Shrugs, then)*: I don't know. The stars weren't aligned? We tried. And now I'm getting a little too old for—

RODNEY: They say you have to want it.

FAY: Bullshit. Ask all the little girls who get pregnant if they wanted—

RODNEY: Want it. And think of it. Picture it. So at the moment of ejaculation, all you've got in your head is: Child-child-child-child. If we'd had a child you wouldn't be like this.

FAY: That is so untrue, that has nothing to do with—

RODNEY: And this wouldn't have happened! Don't you want to be a mother? And you certainly haven't been a very good mother to my child! And I trusted you.

(Short pause.)

I put her in your arms. She was fifteen and I gave her to you to—

FAY: I told you what's happened between us only happened in the last few months—

RODNEY: How do I know that?!! Why should I believe you?!!

(Short pause.)

FAY: I'm sorry. But it's true.

(She stands to pour herself a drink. She takes a sip, sighs:)

Oh God. Eva woke me out of a dream. When she stormed in like that on us. She *stormed in*, you know. As much a memory as a dream actually, 'cause it pretty much happened that way—as in the dream. I was—fourteen? And I had my period. The first one. First time. It happened during the night, in my bed, so there was a stain? I didn't know what to do, but my mother took the sheet and washed it a bit. She hardly seemed to try, I thought, the stain wouldn't come out, so then she hung it outside to dry, in the backyard. It wasn't much of a backyard, tiny, everyone crowded together, yard to yard. Everyone could see—whatever. Everything. That sheet. That stain. Me. I begged my mother not to hang it out there. I cried and begged and pleaded. But she just smiled and said—you'll get used to it.

(Fay, for a moment, is lost in thought, then:)

And then Eva stormed in and woke us up.

(She turns to Rodney. His eyes are closed. She looks at him.)

Are you asleep?

(He doesn't stir. She approaches him to check, and as she gets close, he suddenly shouts. Startled, she screams.)

RODNEY: You pursued me! When Gerald took me backstage, you sat in your dressing room holding your dressing gown tight around your neck like you're so "proper" and "embarrassed," but I look down and it's opened up your leg almost to your ass! You think I didn't know you wanted me to see that?

FAY: I was thirty. I wasn't married. I'd made a decision. Obviously, it was the wrong decision.

RODNEY: Don't say that!! Listen to me. Gerald organized a double date, that's what he said, but later—he told me *you'd* called him to set up—

FAY: I told you I'd made a decision.

RODNEY: And we first slept together in *your* apartment. You kicked your roommate out. I forced you to do nothing.

FAY: I never said you did, Rodney. I never would.

RODNEY: You wanted me. You told me that. You couldn't get enough of me! In your mouth! Inside you!!

FAY: I wanted to get married!! *(Covers her head)* To be married.

(Pause.)

RODNEY: I love you. I love you, Fay. And I wanted you, too. I thought after Betty died I could never give myself again. But you changed that. And I gave myself to you. I held nothing back. What we had maybe wasn't perfect. But it was—good. It was, Fay. Then what happened? What did I do?

FAY: You didn't do anything.

RODNEY: What have I done?!!! You won't even touch me. You
can't even touch me. You think I hadn't noticed?! You think
I'm not human? You think I haven't gone over in my head
a million times: What have I done? What could I do? You
think you're that good an actress that I wouldn't see?!
What?! What can I do?

(Rodney starts to cry. Fay looks at him as he covers his face.)

FAY: I'm sorry. I'm sorry.

RODNEY: Lee's getting married! What about you? You married
me. I'm your husband!

FAY: I know. I know that—

RODNEY: I love you. This will pass. It's something that passes.

FAY: What do you know?

RODNEY: I've watched your face when I've been in you! I know
you! Me! Even if I do disgust you.

FAY: You don't disgust me, Rodney!

RODNEY: No? *(Stares at her, then)* Then come here and show me
that.

FAY: Rodney—

RODNEY: If I don't disgust you, then come here.

*(She hesitates, sets down her drink and goes and sits on the
arm of his chair. He looks up at her, she reaches down and
kisses him on the top of the head. He tries not to sob. He
touches her breast, then rubs it. She lets him.)*

Am I disgusting you?

*(She shakes her head. Then she reaches down and unzips his
pants, unbuckles his belt, wiggles her hand inside his underpants, masturbating her husband. Suddenly he stops her,
and takes her hand out. He tries to stand.)*

Let's go upstairs.

FAY: No.

RODNEY: Let's go upstairs, Fay.
FAY: I can't.

(He stands, trying to hold his pants up.)

RODNEY: Please. Please. Just tonight. Just for one night.

(She shakes her head.)

Let me see your legs. Your legs have always excited me.

(She hesitates, then shows a little leg. He suddenly shouts:)

Don't tease me!
FAY *(Nearly crying)*: I'm not trying to tease you!
RODNEY: Please. It's been too long.

(He goes to her and kisses her on the mouth. He steps back, then kisses her again.)

Too fucking long. Please.

(She looks at him, then:)

FAY: One night. Then that's it. Then something has to happen, Rodney. Do you understand that? Something has to happen.

(He nods, then smiles.)

RODNEY: Come on.
FAY: You understand—
RODNEY: Come on! You first. I want to watch you walk up. I like
    that. Come on.
FAY: Sh-sh.
RODNEY: I don't care who hears. Come on.

(As he follows her off:)

I love you. I do love you.

(They are gone. Off, a dog barks.)

Scene 4

Early next morning. The kitchen.
    Henry finishes writing on a piece of paper. Lee stands next to him.

HENRY: This is the owner. *(Tries to hand her the piece of paper)* He'll fight it, but he owes us back the deposit. We broke nothing.
LEE: Why do I have to do this?
HENRY: Lee, we're leaving. Your father is asking you to do this.

    (She takes the paper.)

    Don't let the owner talk you out of the deposit. Lee?
LEE *(Distracted)*: I won't.
HENRY *(Taking keys out of his pocket)*: And the keys. Your father said you and Ted could have it for the rest of the lease. It's paid for. Why not?
LEE: I don't think so.
HENRY: It's paid for.

LEE: Maybe.

HENRY: Just clean out the refrigerator when you leave.

(Ted enters from the living room.)

TED *(Entering)*: The first taxi's on its way. Somehow it hadn't computed about a second. They're looking for one.

HENRY *(Half to himself, shaking his head)*: "They're looking." Thanks for calling. It's a good thing you thought of—

TED *(To Lee)*: Where have you been?

LEE: Out. Walking.

HENRY: Do they even have a second taxi?

TED: It's coming. It's fine. Where's Eva?

LEE: Outside. She said, making sure a taxi doesn't go by.

HENRY: Even the first one's late.

LEE: What does the word "late" mean here, Henry? Look where you are.

    (To Ted) Henry's given me the keys. I'm supposed to close up.

TED: I'll come back and help.

LEE: Come back?

TED: I'm the only one who knows Italian. I'm going to the airport with them. Your father wants to make sure he gets there.

(Rodney enters from the living room with two large suitcases.)

Let me take those. *(Grabs the suitcases)* The rest are outside—waiting for the taxis.

RODNEY: They're not here yet?

HENRY: Ted says they're coming.

TED: They've been ordered. I was just on the phone. *(As he hurries off outside with the suitcases)* Eva! They're on their way!

RODNEY *(To Lee)*: There you are. Just get up?

LEE: No.

(The phone rings from the living room.)

HENRY: I'll get that.

(He hurries off, leaving Lee and Rodney alone. Awkward pause, neither knows what to say. Then:)

RODNEY: So good morning.

(She nods and tries to smile.)

Are you as tired as I am?

(She shrugs.)

I'll fall asleep like that *("snaps")* on the plane. You going to come back here and stay? I told Henry to— Didn't he say that you and Ted could—?

LEE: He did. He told me. Thank you. I don't know. I'll speak with Ted about it.

RODNEY: Do that.

(He looks at her.)

Lee, he's a— I like him. I think—we're lucky. You'll be happy.

(He takes out his wallet.)

I have all this lira—

LEE: I don't need any money.

RODNEY *(As he holds it out)*: And I'm paying for your apartment. Ted just needs to send me . . . Take it. Take it.

(She takes his money. He looks at her.)

You look so much like your mother.

(He goes to hug her as Fay enters with a little wig box.)

FAY: There's a picture I'd like to have. Where's my camera? Is it
packed?

(Rodney sees a camera on the table and picks it up.)

LEE: That's Henry's.

(Rodney hands Fay the camera.)

You don't know how to use that. And Henry hates anyone
to even touch his camera.

(Awkward moment. Fay sets it back down.)

FAY: Mine must be packed.

(Henry returns.)

HENRY: Problem. The producer. From here. He's heard a rumor.
I don't think those Morris boys can keep their mouths shut.
He's asking me if you're really sick. Or are you leaving?
RODNEY: They told him??
HENRY: I don't know. He's sending a car over to see how you are.
I said I'd see if you were well enough to talk to them. I think
you should.
RODNEY: Now???!
HENRY: He's on the phone.

(Rodney hesitates, looks at Fay and Lee.)

FAY: It'll be all right.

*(She smiles. Then Rodney leads Henry off to the phone in
the living room.)*

74

RODNEY *(Leaving)*: Where's the damn taxi!
HENRY *(To Rodney)*: Now cough a lot into the phone.

(They are gone. Lee and Fay are alone.)

FAY: You're shaking. Are you cold? Here, take my sweater. *(Takes off her sweater and tries to hand it to Lee)*
LEE *(Not taking it)*: You don't have to worry about me.

(Fay picks up the wig box again.)

FAY: My wig that you like so much.
LEE: I like it on you.
FAY: That's what I meant.

(Short pause.)

You're sure you're not cold?
LEE: I hope you have a safe trip back.
FAY: I'm not going—back. I'm going to some other place. Another one. Thank you. And I hope you and . . .
LEE: Stop it. Christ, what could you possibly say that would make me feel better?
FAY: I love you?

(Eva hurries in from outside.)

EVA: A taxi's here! *(Goes and hugs Lee)* Good-bye, dear. I'll miss seeing that sweet face every day.
LEE: Good-bye.
EVA *(Still hugging her)*: I'll write. And you better, too.

(Ted, who has followed Eva in, tries to take Fay's wig box.)

TED: Are you checking this?—
FAY: I'll carry that. There are two big ones still upstairs.

(He goes off to get the suitcases.)

EVA: Where's Rodney?
FAY *(Pointing to the living room)*: Talking on the phone.
EVA *(Hurries off to the living room)*: One taxi's here!

> *(Fay and Lee are again alone. Fay taps the wig box.)*

FAY: I thought of putting this on for you.
LEE: You should have.
FAY: I know.

> *(They look at each other and say nothing. Lee goes and kisses Fay lightly on the lips. They hold each other. Rodney, Henry and Eva enter.)*

HENRY *(To Rodney)*: That was very convincing.

> *(Rodney "coughs.")*

EVA: Why were you coughing?
RODNEY: We'll tell you later. Who's in the first taxi?
FAY *(Holding on to Lee's arm)*: Henry, take our picture. Me and Lee.

> *(Short awkward moment, no one knows what to do, then:)*

EVA: There isn't time, Fay.
RODNEY: She's right. There isn't. Who's in the first taxi?
EVA: You and Fay. I told him to put most of the luggage in with you. Get that there first—I thought—
HENRY: Good idea.

> *(Fay slowly lets Lee go. Henry goes to shake hands with Lee.)*

Good-bye.

LEE *(As they shake)*: Good-bye.

HENRY: And congratulations again.

LEE *(Confused)*: For what?

(Eva laughs.)

EVA: Your engagement!

(Rodney goes to say good-bye to Lee.)

RODNEY: Good-bye.

(They hug.)

EVA: Everyone take something—

RODNEY: Wait. Why don't you ride with me?

(This change of plan stops everyone.)

LEE: To the airport? I didn't know I was going to the airport?

RODNEY *(Holding her face)*: I'm not going to see you for such a long time. We can say good-bye there. Fay?

FAY: Go. Go.

LEE: Is there room?

RODNEY: Fay?

FAY: I'll wait for the next . . .

(Ted enters with the two suitcases.)

LEE: Ted, Dad wants me to go to the airport to see him off.

TED: Why not? We'll take a taxi back.

RODNEY *(To no one)*: I think I just don't want to say good-bye.

EVA: You should go. Go on.

RODNEY: He's waiting. Let's go.

EVA: Do we know where to meet?

RODNEY: Henry knows.

(Rodney leads Lee off.)

EVA *(As a hint to Henry)*: Do you need some help with those, Ted?
HENRY: Whose suitcases are—?
EVA: It doesn't matter, does it?
FAY *(To herself, distracted)*: They're mine.
EVA: Do you need help, Ted?
HENRY: Let me help.
TED: I'm fine.

(As Eva, Henry and Ted leave:)

EVA: Henry, you should be helping . . .

(As they go, Lee hurries back past them. Fay suddenly sees her.)

LEE: I thought I better take a sweater.

(She takes Fay's sweater.)

FAY: Good idea.

(Lee starts to go, stops.)

LEE: Aren't you . . . *("going outside")*
FAY: I'll wait in here. They'll call me.
LEE: See you at the . . .
FAY: We'll say good-bye there.

(Lee nods and hurries off. Fay is alone. She hugs her wig box and sits. Then she has a thought, and she starts to unzip the box. She looks around for a mirror, then hurries off into the living room. Henry and Ted return.)

HENRY: Is that everything?
TED: I'll call the taxi company again.

HENRY: Give it a couple of minutes. *(Big sigh)* You should have seen him on the phone, Rodney. He was very convincing.

(He "coughs.")

TED: I don't understand. Why did he have to pretend?
HENRY: I called in sick for him this morning. He was due on the set at seven. You forget what a small town this is. I don't know what they heard, but— Well, we're on our way home.

(Eva hurries in.)

EVA: It's the other taxi! *(Hurries out)*
HENRY *(As they start to leave)*: We haven't forgotten anything?
TED: I've checked all the rooms. Twice. Everything's outside.
HENRY *(Hesitates)*: You're sure?
TED: I'm sure. Come on, let's go.
HENRY: Okay.

(They start to go.)

I still feel like we're forgetting something.

(They are gone. Fay returns, wearing her blond wig. She goes back to her seat, oblivious that the others have left, and waits. Long pause. Lights fade.
Woman of the Prologue speaks to the audience:)

WOMAN: It took Mom a good twenty minutes before she realized she'd been forgotten. And Henry, Eva and Ted drove a good mile in the taxi before they realized they'd left Mom behind and turned around. And on their way to the airport everyone pretended as if nothing had happened.

Mom flew back to America with Dad, with whom she'd live for the rest of her life. She never saw Lee again after that day. Lee did get married, but soon divorced, and never married again. Her Christmas cards, which Mom saved religiously, were signed by both Lee and a friend, Elizabeth.

Six weeks later, in some doctor's office in L.A., Mom learned that she was pregnant with me. Conceived I was that night in my parents' bedroom in a small villa on the edge of Rome.

Of my birth, Mom wrote in her diary: "Maybe this baby will make everything all right."

(Short pause.)

My mom died when I was eighteen. She died again when I was twenty, twenty-eight, thirty-six; she died again just this week when I forgot a look in her eye that I thought I would remember for the rest of my life. And I suppose she'll go on dying until one day I'll close my eyes and won't be able to see any of her, anymore.

And she'll be gone. Forgotten—by everyone.

Her name—was Fay.

But for as long as I can remember, she was known—as Rodney's wife.

END OF PLAY

RICHARD NELSON's plays include *Frank's Home, Rodney's Wife, Franny's Way, Goodnight Children Everywhere, New England, Some Americans Abroad, Two Shakespearean Actors, Madame Melville, The General from America, Misha's Party* (with Alexander Gelman), *Columbus and the Discovery of Japan, Left, Principia Scriptoriae, Life Sentences, Between East and West* and *The Vienna Notes.* His adaptations include *Tynan* (with Colin Chambers, based on *The Diaries of Kenneth Tynan*); Jean-Claude Carriere's *The Controversy*; Strindberg's *Miss Julie* and *The Father*; Chekhov's *The Cherry Orchard, Three Sisters, The Seagull* and *The Wood Demon*; Pirandello's *Enrico IV*; Fo's *Accidental Death of an Anarchist* and Beaumarchais's *The Marriage of Figaro.* He has written the musicals: *James Joyce's The Dead* (with Shaun Davey) and *My Life with Albertine* (with Ricky Ian Gordon); the screenplay for the film *Ethan Frome*; and the book *Making Plays* (with David Jones).

He has received numerous awards both in America and abroad, including a Tony Award (Best Book of a Musical for *James Joyce's The Dead*), an Olivier award (Best Play for *Goodnight Children Everywhere*), Tony nominations (Best Play for *Two Shakespearean Actors*; Best Score as co-lyricist for *James Joyce's The Dead*), an Olivier nomination (Best Comedy for *Some Americans Abroad*), two Obies, a Lortel Award, a New York Drama Critics Circle Award, a Guggenheim Fellowship and a Lila Wallace-Reader's Digest Writers Award. He is an Honorary Associate Artist of The Royal Shakespeare Company, and Chair of the Playwriting Department of the Yale School of Drama. He lives in upstate New York.